HISTORIES HAUNT US

Histories Haunt Us

ꟹ

Triny Finlay

NIGHTWOOD EDITIONS
GIBSONS, BC
2010

Nightwood Editions
P.O. Box 1779
Gibsons, BC VON 1VO
Canada
www.nightwoodeditions.com

TYPESETTING: Carleton Wilson
COVER DESIGN: Anna Comfort
COVER ART: "As Above So Below" by Alexandra Eldridge

Nightwood Editions acknowledges financial support from the Government of Canada through the Book Publishing Industry Development Program and the Canada Council for the Arts, and from the Province of British Columbia through the British Columbia Arts Council and the Book Publisher's Tax Credit.

This book has been produced on 100% post-consumer recycled, ancient-forest-free paper, processed chlorine-free and printed with vegetable-based dyes.

Printed and bound in Canada

LIBRARY AND ARCHIVES CANADA CATALOGUING IN PUBLICATION

Finlay, Triny, 1976–
Histories haunt us / Triny Finlay.

Poems.
ISBN 978-0-88971-247-8

I. Title.

PS8611.I65H58 2010 C811'.6 C2010-901128-7

For my family

and in memory of my great-grandmother, Clara Strang

HISTORIES HAUNT US

NEW ASTRONOMERS

New Astronomers

Fear is passed on like the colour of eyes,
the texture of hair. You know this.

—Susan Goyette, *The True Names of Birds*

Return is inevitable because we need something
To define ourselves against…

—Matthea Harvey, *Pity the Bathtub Its Forced Embrace of the Human Form*

ABSTRACT LOSS, I

Two hours from John Thompson's cross
in Jolicure, two hours from a second storey.

Twitchy all day, sorting tiles for a mosaic,
searching for a rosary-style rite.

Flowers in slim vases, no shotguns.
Purple orchids slumped like shamed teenagers,

turning away from each other, turning away.
Yellow mums remind me of my son.

And down my arm in everlasting ink
the sweep, the clean lines of Mucha's yarrow.

ABSTRACT LOSS, 2

Someone else's Grammy saying,
Please God
Oh please God please.

No children under four.

Here's to Tony Soprano—I'm catching up on the violence.

And alone in this, my room;

uneasy soul, chafing
she stops at my door:
You fellers aren't hiding a dog in there,
are you?

For the line, for the arc, for the buffered edge, I think
I'll find my way back. There are words I've known,
how water makes things happen.

White, red ochre, dirty mauve and blue: the pills
scored and mashed inside, what future joy—

the faithful dog shall bear her company.

ABSTRACT LOSS, 3

My family at the glass doors.

An army vet walks by, shoots me with:
    Excuse me, do you know those people?

Thirteen-year-old version of me, cracked and cradled
in afghans, extra firm sofa, willing escape.

But not leaving, no angel's wing, no fire.

Hands smoothed by brown paper towel; darkening roots; breasts
stretched and squeezed and suddenly leaking milk.

Reaching for that gap, that equal sky.

Comfort: bread and bread enough for all.

ABSTRACT LOSS, 4

I want neutral words for this, like
table
music
soft
child.

But it all comes at once, a gypsy's warning:

off at the side, the wall, my gourd, my head, my nut, my tree,
  my trolley
round the twist, the bend, coco, harpic.

We've come as we are, red
from the day's driving rain
and one last roll in the hay.

We've been taken out of time.

Won't sing like a katydid chorus, won't laugh
but ready for the last, ecstatic trumpet blast.

ABSTRACT LOSS, 5

It begins again, eighth day of watermelon chewing gum
Sanka in tangerine packets, all singles.

Someone's fine-tuned hummingbird tattoo
pills and group and pills and group and pills.

This is a public unveiling.

A clot, a break in the loop.

The shock of automatic toilets, sinks,
no tubs, no pipes exposed
no leverage.

Remove the desk lamp.
Remove the glass vases, the tweezers, the clippers—
a vague future in welts and shards, electrical cords.

Lights out, every night, staring at the gap
between the door and the reinforced door jamb.

THE THAW THAT WINTER YOU WENT CRAZY

In that town on the marsh with the school on the hill, poets who haunt first editions, stairwells. Whispered apocrypha. First the man with the red fleece sweatshirt who followed you on errands: the post office. Groceries. Sign to you of a mounting plague. Mould spreading ceiling to wall, wall to edges of bed. The inevitable itch. Pushing furniture in the dead of the night, a desk chair that must not face south. Bedbugs and lotions for lice. Hospital visits. The marsh freezes for hockey but we skate toward the highway, past the waterfowl lookouts, the last house. That's the way it was in that town. We balance on wooden rails, new astronomers, rye swelling our veins and clouding the air we fall against, fall into. First the intensity of ice, then the thaw. And everywhere. Stories from Ontario of trucks going through the lake and down here we're busiest in our heads, fishtailing, talking a blue streak as if words might steer you away from the cracking, from slipping between the boards, or drowning.

SELF-PORTRAIT AS CANNONBALL

Sits in Officer's Square
lodged in that great black throat
so cold and guttural.

Somewhere else a smoker's lung collapses.

Rough metal held by the hands of small
children seeking adventure.

Endurance.

Gravity doesn't always let us down.

THAT PRIMAL SAMENESS

Thirst
that first night of spring
in a red-brick town.

Something we find and hold
between us: martini glass,
olive pick, dry ice.

Backyard cigarettes, neighbours
flicking porch lights off and on
in protest.

Men who drink too much, incriminate
themselves at cocktail parties, drive home
after scuffles over driving home.

Women who take extra care
with the placement of bobby pins, a flush
painted on.

The quiet cling of velvet to those ribs.

Coupling, or the obverse; of
not seeking this now, or ever, this
pairing off like fetal cells.

Those who missed the abstract proof between us
and those who picked at it, wanted a cut.

Wanting a cut and, parched, forgetting the thaw.

A look we might have missed, in a different room.

Inhaling without reason, taking
in smoke, the fumes of gin and other flaws
that persevere, trace on your arm at the true end
of the day—breathing the future in particles.

THAT CAVERNOUS QUESTION

I.

The house is made of rotted wood,
which we can only know through destruction.

This is no more than a hole
to hide out in.

The finest art can be the ugliest metaphor,
loaded, fired against the walls
(and Plato ugliest of all).

We have all been pinned for exhibition
or reduced to a single pixel-point, trapped
in an unrelenting room.

2.

But Jesus could you ever
go back to that place
he had you believe exists,

hanging used bras
on bronze sculptures of soldiers.

It's a space you broke out of.

It's a paperweight.

There were worn-out music boxes and cans of drying paint
but never any shadows on the wall.

SELF-PORTRAIT AS THE SPANISH CIVIL WAR

Freeze me, frame me, hang me in the air
like the horse in Picasso's painting.

Suspended in space and time, lyric
as a moth, loved by the lepidopterist.

I am the horror of war, a severed
limb still hanging onto the sword.

Faith sticks. A mother holds a limp
child, looks down on the earth. I will too.

Words would mean nothing here—
I can't speak for the merciless.

Holding on, but we can't frame this.
I am black and white, grotesque, frail,

I fail at hope, falling through
the floor of a burning building.

OF ANY CHORUS

I.

Took my own tongue, stuffed in a jar,
and carried it home to find you.

Took my own tongue for a ferry ride
and watched you trail behind.

2.

Make it of wind if the weather is fine

make it of fire if the doves die

make it of water if depth is the issue

make it of pleasure
          of parasites

pray.

3.

Took my own tongue to the river's edge
while the rain set up its trespass.

Took my own tongue to the baker's house
and sat by the open oven.

SELF-PORTRAIT AS SOMEONE YOU MIGHT LIKE TO MEET

Because I like to arrange pills in patterns
before I take them.

Because there are no elephants here.

Because I've mentioned elephants.

I was broken—I'll say it plain
and that's what you'll like,
the plainness, smooth
face, pop of blue in the eye.

I read 'til I was green again
(new and ill and envious).
It didn't work but I kept going.

The words weren't enough
and neither is this.

CONTACT

We will say one thing
and mean something else.

There will be a gap
this time, imperfections—

dreams will keep us
separate: half here in the perfect
bed, half with the sallow self
in a stand of poplars, calling.

There is a saint
for this landscape
and, blind in the snow,
I will shield the baby.

The one in the bed
will hide, miss steps toward
preservation (forget sugar, forget light),
exclude the other half.

The earth cannot hold
its bile in any solid form;
I will choke with the trees.

Each gland lends me some protection from loss.

WHISPERING WALL

Catch me, catch me
lolling into the tiles,

faint with you and newlywed echoes,
vaulting one small word to the other side.

By the oyster bar at Grand Central Station
I skipped you a secret, standing, facing

the subway-tiled wall. We found it in a book,
this honeymoon game, a novelty act

we perform midday, knowing no one.
August, and next we'll search

for the hidden bar, where writers met
and talked and shocked, protected.

But now I want you to catch my call—
a simple sound for two. That ceiling hears

all, steals voices.

but hangs on.

At first not tangible, not even
lingering like burnt salmon
in the kitchen.

Then surfacing in a small framed print
in the foyer, watching
our coming, every departure

(but not as knick-knack, not
devil's ivy, not
coffee-table book).

Hangs on as if hanging
could matter, could navigate the stale March air
and heal, bring us back to that other joy.

Hangs on and coaxes forgetting,

hangs on, an absent
friend whose soul sits
in a chair on the screened-in porch.

SELF-PORTRAIT AS RUBENESQUE FIGURE

I could come to you in a dream—you can handle
the anachronistic journey, inevitability:

Wearing nothing but a fur wrap, I'm a pastoral landscape.
You're the lonely shepherd.

Surprise me with your sunken lid.
Exhume me. I've fermented.

I wanted a trip back in time. I was a goddess:
dimpled knees; navel deep with spice.

If you could take me like this
you would; unveil me

after so many cloistered
months, the lady will not reveal her secrets,
knotted toe pointing out beyond the frame.

FUTURE COSMETICS

What they might try to map out
on my face when I die; or with needles.

I would rather burn.

The unfinished quilts
pressed, in a case, beneath the bed

some still uncut and, so, whole.

But waiting.

Of floral wreaths, lily stench, baskets lined
like seniors' beds with impermeable sheets.

And the pale dog, lost now, somewhere pleased
or desperate, wondering.

That last drink drawn between us.

An imperceptible surge in the grid, in
the walls that hide our wiring.

FEBRUARY

Another look
at how the mind imagines space.

We are taught to separate words
with gaps, or no words, first
using a finger as measure,
then our eyes

and depth perception
and habit.

February is always
the shortest kid in the class:
pale, ready for a fight.

Calls you an asshole like he means it, like
it's your first name

but copies your spelling homework:
pride
sliver
sensitivity.

Later he waits tables while you read
everything; he waits for others.

But now he is this small, freckled self, cruel
and angry, someone you always come back to.

WHAT IS CUT OR NEGATIVE

I.

After the bliss of the baby came the flies.

The city, the garbage ripe,
in heat beneath our kitchen window.

They cruised through a hole
in the screen and gathered,
a buzz of watchful parishioners.

2.

We went to movie theatres, synchronized
our focus, a small and striking agreement.

Ate lentils in airy cafés while the baby, strapped
to my burgeoning chest, slept.

Eavesdropped on bearded men dissecting
Ang Lee in detail:
    what prescient directives he gives,
    what must have been cut to carve out
    that antique Elinor or, later, Ennis.

But we can't see the wreckage.

3.

After the flies we started eating
meat again, not a conscious
choice, but to build a temple out of bone.

And what we see in celluloid—
tightly wound but gradually unspooling—
will wrap itself around my riven core.

WHAT PASSES BETWEEN

In our living room, nothing
as trite as tension.

Bluegrass on the stereo
and warm air shooting up from
the floor; the baby tired but rolling
toward Etobicoke.

We were going to order in, stuck
on the next move, muted menus laid
out on the oak table.

Ground down by stories we couldn't hear:
two extra bodies in the house and nothing
new or to be known.

By eight-fifteen we were running
out of the better beer and the women
didn't want any more white wine.

We must all have been
willing the thing—that quiver between
them, that cruel elephant—to die,
to be taken outside, or stop playing.

But eight-thirty came and went, the baby
fell asleep on my shoulder, and we ate nothing.

SELF-PORTRAIT AS THE LONG WAY

And in the front a cowgirl, a cowboy
no horses
no ropes
no loops
no ties
no sense of how the late summer sun will shine.

And in the backseat, he's three years old
taking it all in
fists full of loaders and semis and heavy haulers.

BEING SO CAREFUL

—after Frank Davey's "The Mirror"

And, so, tied to it.

That careful.

The litany of names we chant
low in the throat while we do
other things with the body
(tying garbage bags every Wednesday
morning, tying shoelaces too loosely).

The list of everyone we've slept with
(revised, reduced, rendered)—never
written down, though once we tried,
each letter angled the wrong
way, moving backwards.

The list of names we like
for a girl baby
    a boy baby
and over and over
we sing them from the feet
up, testing buoyancy.

Being so careful
with the water we drink
and wash with, the comfort
of plainness.

What we know of purity.

We are tied to it,
to apron strings
    purse strings
            rings on our fingers.

The names we are calling without speaking.

The snake plant, commonly called mother-in-law's
tongue, fails most easily when overwatered.

This garden is dry-lipped, growing liver spots.

I enter laughing, fuck-me boots
and that teal leather trench coat,
popping in on the way out

(describe the Indian meal we will eat downtown,
describe the route to get there).

A series of overnight stays on the sofa bed, canned
peas and demanding diet queries

(describe vegetarianism).

Watching *The Truman Show* without irony; early to bed.

A series of escapes, first ours

(describe your friend's newborn, describe the
drugstore errand)

then hers

(describe a typical day, describe any medications,
palpitations, indications).

Lose the present tense

(describe how you met your sweetheart and how you
met your sweetheart).

Leave a record

(describe Goya if for wars).

Cancel everything: the wedding the birth the dress
you were going to wear the night nurse the cleaning and
cleaning the way you wear your hair.

Lose the certainty of time, lose time, purge on every level

(describe furniture, the camel painting, toaster ovens,
other small appliances).

Take it back, take it back and leave us with you.

FALLING

Make this a study of gravity.

Make it move
like the plates in the soft, tiny skull.

Like a landless landslide.

There will be warnings—weeks
maybe; there will be pain.

Drink water.
Do not eat.
Tell someone you love.

Make it loose without cracking
                    without this fault-line pressure
          with or without needles, or pining.

This is the first fact
a closeness with no closure
(a riptide breaking).

Make this a true 'either/or':
                    descends/doesn't
                         tears/doesn't
                    breathes/doesn't.

Make this nothing like disaster
(but after
or after

PHOBIC

How not to be obsessed with progress.

The fear of panic for no precise reason
                the mind's inability to process
                concepts
                simple as panic.

The son who built bridges but dreamt
            of swallowing the sea—
                motor skills crumbled
                heart lost pace.

His hands are my hands.

Of the gaps between what really happens
and what to grasp from
those gaps between.

Or his mother, so blue she went to bed one night
and stayed there, a ghost quartet
of clever boys settled on the stairs.

Said *Goodnight* and meant it, *Goodnight*
for seventeen years then off to a levelled life
in Montreal.

Her mouth so perfect in portraits,
her spellbound eyes.

The fear of ghosts, the sharp tear
of nothing, dead skin
still attached to a breathing body.

The train that went by
but you can't tell which way
by looking at the tracks.

PRESTIDIGITATION

For my next trick I will devastate all insects.

I'll begin with what I have always known
as potato bugs, though they're called
something useful around here.

Then I'll move on to earwigs, centipedes, ants that bite

and the cosmic range of those in flight.

And balconies
potted plants
flimsy window screens
patio doors
knives in blocks
heavy televisions
earrings

paper.

Another trick will involve jealous cats and cribs
but I can't explain the subtleties here.

Another turns junk mail into edible oil products;
another conquers carcinogens (but not cancer).

I will need a volunteer.

Histories Haunt Us

The small stone in my hand weighs years:
it is dark.

To turn, and remember, that
is the fruit.

—John Thompson, *Stilt Jack*

(i)

And your nose an emperor, I can't get over your, your
perfectly perfect streamlined aquiline nose. This must

be love. Coffee with milk, instant, between us at midnight
though eventually I'll buy a French press. What keeps

us laughing, leavening, fastening—skating downtown,
falling on your ass and liking it, to show us how it

might be, this ice; bread you kneaded for our son
when it had to be home-made; banana smoothies

before supper. Playing at construction sites and car
crash scenes, truck after truck beneath our feet

and still you can do the voice of each character. I bear
witness. *Imagination meets memory in the dark.*

(ii)

Back to a line I repeat to myself
wasting time, messing it up for nothing.

This process of future, moving rocks around
as if we were gods of perseverance.

Moving it, our breath a loop
like the diligent clarinetist

who taught himself to move it
in a circle. Not reeds or boulders

but a breath. I am that musician, trying
to find the one continuous line.

Until the missing story is told,
nothing besides: we shall go on quietly craving it.

(iii)

Chew it in 4/4 time, this list of offences.
A lion for a day, not a sheep.

To say it, that you betrayed me
with backyard kisses and me running

home to find somebody, other, in our bed.
It was February, nearly time for the one

train to leave town. I thought she was
on it already. Instead, her kitten nipples

peering out at me as I rounded the corner
thinking, at last, to press you under

my thumbs. I was a pink, gaping mouth.
Kept the house key, turned back, didn't cut you off.

(iv)

Desire for, desire for, desire for the story: *it happens*
in a sequence of time but finds its own order…

I've only understood causality once or twice
in my life: pregnancy; under the knife.

If we move suddenly in the open-air jeep
the feasting lions might lose sight

of their humbled impala. This a line, a fixing,
a process of suture. One thing leads to another

and now a baby, a scar, a photo of the pride
from only a few night-strokes away.

Straight from the past. Now intervene—
the continuous thread of revelation.

(v)

Every idea borrowed, and this, and before this,
watch faces, voices, gestures, moods, survive

through cunning. It starts as a subtle fear,
immobilizes. Takes me from the quick strides

of a walk downtown to paralysis.
I was a droplet of water on a wheel

and I stayed like this, like this, my lips
stretched taut as a tire and you lashed out.

When I said nothing it did not mean consent.
When I burst back you knew what I meant.

This is it now. You slashed and I spun.
The weight of the silence will choke us.

(vi)

Flesh of my flesh. Another beginning.
Late apple season in the Valley.

Histories haunt us. The bees with their honey
have kept us in sweetness and light. Neighbours

heave firewood in through the basement
window, I've watched the begonias die.

Bodies are facts that multiply, the squirrels
eat rotting pumpkins, and we walk on

because of the rhythms of trees. Our small
boy gathers desiccated maple leaves to bring

into the house, to stay warm. Winter
comes like an idiot babbling, and strewing flowers.

(vii)

Gather rosehips for tea. You've been lonely
before and the memory might have you isolate.

There are wars we've never seen, not beyond
pixel-mist TV images or a line in someone else's

poem. This war is like being trapped in a dryer, like
someone's missing cat, twitchy and ravenous.

You're in a room in town, the heat is set high.
Waiting for a knock at the door. In another time,

the subway doors chimed as they closed; now
school buses send children to the country. Muscles

cramp as your body tries to adjust,
to remember, to sift, to weigh, to estimate.

(viii)

How many more poems about love and houseplants
to believe that what is true for you is true.

One man gilds fast-food coffee spoons for display
until McDonald's stops making the plastic molds:

too many tools for too much blow. I used to crave
flour, raw, the mulch of it in my mouth, the worms

that were promised by my mother. The secret to winter
is combing coppery hair in low light, sipping

peppermint tea from a clay mug. The heft of the mug,
spark of fire in the strands, building a handbook

to the present. I wanted to write a short talk on beauty,
wanted to hide and sound like somebody else.

(ix)

If the builder has learned from his father how
to raise a house with bare hands, how

to find a girl and fuck her with no thought
of boundaries. No boundaries, but a Protestant work ethic.

Maybe it's a pattern I needed to learn, the builders
with their fetishes, never stopping before the house

is complete. Mouths ripe with spring's infinite charms,
with cold sores. So many hands digging into me

like dull-edged trowels, like the welder's arc
that mustn't be watched. I have to admit I looked,

looked at the arc every time: a solar eclipse,
a gradual oozing away through the years.

(x)

Jumping from step to step, down, just jumping.
Before I knew to think critically I was only a judge

of pleasure. The street-sweeper swishes and quishes
and drones. I delight in the white noise of it

brushing the dust away, my oak-leaf broom.
And the small boy, too, is rapt when it's his turn

to be swept away by a simple machine. We've
been watching him sleep on a pile of books,

splitting the bindings with the weight of his fresh
mind, or waiting at the oven for oatmeal cookies

that will soften in his mouth like untrained ice.
The soul's duty, the soul's duty: it must abandon itself.

(xi)

Knuckles dried out from electric heat, a shift
to my childhood brain, *to not regret, to not look back*

or satisfy reversion. For years I hid in my closet,
literally: blankets for rugs, shelves for a desk

and a radio for top 100, for ball games, George Bell
battling it out again with Saberhagen. Endless review.

The warmth of the cocoon but really it's: Dear God—
I'm going to hell for thinking this—I want you to smite

me, to take me out of this shade. Self-conscious
and praying for it. Going back. Eleven (Bell's tag,

my age) became my lucky number. And now to worry
the waste, the waste of energy, for wallowing.

(xii)

Listing like a junkie against you, against
my mother. Along Dundas at 4 am, past

the precinct. Harsh tea from Tim Horton's
as I slope into the garbage bin, wracked

out of the promise of the real. I knew it would
start like this but what do we know before

we are stricken—spikes on a graph
telling us when the baby is feeling

ready. Ice chips, the tiny coil of metal
wound into the tiny head so we can quantify

the heart's design. Vacuum extraction. *Planets,*
lives, dirt, rocks. You get tired, you lose the pattern.

(xiii)

My surprise, Oh my surprise, on watching him emerge,
my son, *and sings the tune without words and never stops.*

We are all so open in this, our sounds so guttural, a glow
in the throat, in the flow, his Moro reflex, not really

falling. It's such a cliché to say I don't recall
the pain, but I can't defend what the body

remembers. First I lay so still on my side, every movement
pinching the cord, and then you were out in the world

your own lusty aria, wiped of blood and the vernix
earned in the womb, an unquiet bed made for you.

Comerado, I give you my hand, my breast
to share your bliss, slick from the passage.

(xiv)

Not for this anxiety, not for this, but
trying to put a quart in a pint cup.

Our son back at the hospital. Different this time:
seizures, swollen joints, vasculitis. For a few minutes

of each day he goes blind, finds my face with his hands.
For days and nights I am awake, ready for the nurses'

hourly calls, or trying to lie like a snake, coiling
around my sleeping husband. Later, it subsides

while in Fredericton the river's spilling out into the grid,
kayaks reel down Brunswick St., pumps yield.

These things encroach, they devastate, so that
you must decide: you are an anchor or you are not.

(xv)

Once the fledglings had stumbled home flushed
from the wind's abuse, once it meant something

to mix rye, to tell a lie and to be held accountable.
By seventeen I was opening up, a windstorm, opening

out into that small town with the marsh and the hill
and the rye. Played out the love triads, caught,

released, caught, released, a small perch to rest on.
Needed a church of my own beyond pool and bar

and school—a dry apse—to be saved from my lapses
in prudence. But only the pond, the snowed paths,

dusty flowers, the clank of censers
and tracks, leading from somewhere to nowhere.

(xvi)

Powder room, Saskatoon, rethinking my cobalt
life. *It silts up exactly like silt in a flowing stream.*

In a stall, in limbo, listening in on another
existence. Now, *to go where I've never been.*

To think that this might progress beyond
a hotel toilet—some people call it voiding

or emptying, so a void: a mis-marriage, one
to come; shunning you at a hostel in Paris

because of the sounds of your sleep. It seems
mean, this talk, as if I wished for abject desires

and escape from small rooms I've owned.
Oh, friends, *our place knows us no more.*

(xvii)

Quick with a needle, like Mennonite quilters
to fix me. Just stretch me over a good wooden frame

and sew. I've been worked before like that strong
cotton fabric, sliced, pieced, and sliced again—

find the eye, the seam, the gap, the ditch.
Or maybe you are the taxidermist, handling the bird

that is my core; I edged my way down the great
spruce and now you mould me with clay, size me,

fill me with my own double. It can't go on,
this lesson in cut and paste. I bleed. I need

to trade in my glass eyes, my appliqué, to ride
the wind of the wing of madness.

(xviii)

Restless on a plane to Toronto, pumped full
of Ativan. The stewardess isn't far beyond

this: touching up lip gloss, hairpin; pocket mirror,
cellphone scroll. The form and where to put it.

Our son throws up, still I tremble, shift the crossed
leg to the other side. You're sopping it up

with stiff paper towel and some extra sick-bags.
I turn my head away, rub my knees, descend.

It's not that I'm oblivious to what generates, what
keeps it all going. Energy from within and a few

pearl buttons. I've found my ways to set down,
to escape—*adornment nothing but a reflection.*

(xix)

Seven years, and now in the silver car, *not because*
it is righteous or noble, not because it seems good

but a trip made round, Toronto to Fredericton, back
to where we started together. That perfect loaf of bread.

We've brought it with us, crossing Québec once, west
and now the other way, three of us this time, so much

devotion. Cucumber slices liquefy in clear plastic
containers, cartons and cartons of rice milk, detours

for friends along the way. We won't drive in the dark
this time, we're older, more afraid. Soon we'll stop

for deer, soon we'll light, kiss in the dusk, here now
because we must and not in any other way.

(xx)

Take the farmers in Eritrea, suicidal from the drought
and I only know them because of my cab driver.

In Australia, too, they're leaving us, no rain. No key
to the cattle, no barley grain. And here, some of us

are also trying to go, to suffer our exposure
to the world. There was a time when sunlight

was enough, when oceans sustained us. Ours
was a fair landscape, an equal field. But this

is a myth too, the myth of progress reversed.
We suffer, but we are not land to be elegized.

That was a time when only the dead
could smile. This is a verb instead of a noun.

(xxi)

Unlikely, I know, but what if we're keeping track
of the wrong ideas, the one with the record book

walking and walking and gone. Freedom was
my first typewriter, Olympia, sitting alone

in the white-walled basement, waiting for me.
Quiet but for the whine and click, I went for

the rhyme, Byron on the brain in the late eighties.
And boys Oh boys to start, unrequited love,

peace like a dove and anything on my mind.
A fantasy game, songs for the forgotten, letters

never sent. I spent that time in excesses: *wanna fly,*
you got to give up the shit that weighs you down.

(xxii)

Vaguely, just vaguely, from my point of view: into
the book about red, for the world about flight, about red

running out, or growing wings, volcano-like, monstrous.
The colour of delirium. It was Valentine's Day, though

nothing to me. I'd been stashing pills for a week, some
from everyone. No trust in myself, no snow, weak

at the throat, so dry from the forced air heat, so dry
from the chalky Tylenol—I'll never take it again.

And so a tumbler of water, that's what saved me. Sip
after sip after each tiny pill and they drowned. But

just vaguely, beginning with this, my confession,
to calm, to calm, to calm an impetuous tide.

(xxiii)

Waved through at customs, eyeballed, scanned, and swiped
and a large man emerges from an airtight room, escorted,

hands dangling at an odd angle, the brief glint of chain
under a coat that hangs between his arms, cloaked.

This is control, maybe the state, Toronto to Houston
to Puebla. He is rushed through security, feet barely

touch ground, and he's gone. In the departures lounge
a middle-aged woman ripping pages from *Reader's Digest*,

just scanning and ripping, collecting each paper to tear.
Rapt, I wonder who will sit with me on the flight.

A long trip alone, *changeable, fitful and maddening.*
You were once wild here. Two towers and a pyramid.

(xxiv)

Xanthos on a picture card in his room, since birth.
Words I never knew except for him. At a wedding

one September we find new friends from Israel,
linguists who fall for his thriving mind. Teach us

melafefon! melafefon!—Hebrew for cucumber—and
on and on, the patter with the funniest sounds they can

name. I did this too, my Saturday morning brain,
Les Stromphes, my mum's Franglais. Before he rode a trike

he sang, *I got soul but I'm not a sol-jah!* into a makeshift
mike, mimed my father's speech at another wedding.

Now we are deaf and numb. *Mushi mushi*, into the toy
phone. *I won't lose all the other ages I've been.*

(xxv)

Years after the floods, and after consequence;
dying is a wild night and a new road.

I thought it would bleed out, that it would be fine
leaving stains settling into the hardwood.

Caught with the knife, midair, confessing
the big, bruised secrets and filing each one away,

despair so organized. It's easier on Sundays
when we're all slowly leaking anyway.

Take it in; leave it to the stale air. We've been
there before, we know how to communicate. Fill

a pine box with the nuts you can't tolerate.
Do not laugh. Do not let me negotiate.

(xxvi)

Zero degree I am, and craving iron: the cedars bent
by the wind. The wind. Some fell. Counting that

means nothing—some fell—but we're watching from
inside, pouring cups of steaming chai, late afternoon.

The truth is that I fell too, feel as helpless as the trees
and I won't disguise it anymore in metaphor. Someone

sent me a postcard of a bird on a limb, calligraphic
swirls in the background. It was February (back

to that month) and I should tell that friend: in
February a bird on a limb is a gift shared, well-

earned. The truth is, it stings, it sings to me now.
The falling leaves return to the ground.

NOTES ON THE POEMS

The last line of "Abstract Loss, 2" revises a line from Alexander Pope's *An Essay On Man.*

"That Primal Sameness" is a love song for Drew Kennickell, as is (i) in "Histories Haunt Us."

"Self-Portrait as the Spanish Civil War" alludes to Ken Babstock's "What We Didn't Tell the Medic."

"Self-Portrait as Rubenesque Figure" alludes to Rubens's painting "Helena Fourment in a Fur Wrap" ("Het Pelsken"), c. 1638.

"Histories Haunt Us" glosses the work of many writers. Ghosts include:

(i) Annie Dillard; (ii) T.S. Eliot and Laura Riding; (iii) Elizabeth Henry; (iv) Eudora Welty; (v) Marge Piercey and Audre Lorde; (vi) Edna St. Vincent Millay; (vii) Tillie Olsen; (viii) Ralph Waldo Emerson; (ix) Jack London; (x) Rebecca West; (xi) Katherine Mansfield; (xii) Ursula K. Le Guin; (xiii) Emily Dickinson and Walt Whitman; (xiv) Charlotte Perkins Gilman; (xv) Anna Akhmatova; (xvi) May Sarton, Diane Arbus and Victor Hugo; (xvii) Charles Baudelaire; (xviii) Coco Chanel; (xix) Ursula K. Le Guin; (xx) Anna Akhmatova and Ulysses S. Grant; (xxi) Toni Morrison; (xxii) Mary Wollstonecraft; (xxiii) May Sarton and Isadora Duncan; (xxiv) The Killers and Madeline L'Engle; (xxv) Emily Dickinson.

ACKNOWLEDGEMENTS

My thanks to: Silas White, for more grounding and insights; Madeline Bassnett, Matt Holmes, Anita Lahey, Sharon McCartney and Rob Winger for all things, poetic and otherwise; Catherine Chapman, Tracia Finlay, Jody Mason, Jan Purnis and Ella Soper-Jones for the love and lady-talk; Jane Higgins, Carole Lamarche and Nancy Morin for showing me the way home; and Sherry & Tom Finlay, Tamara Finlay, and Tracy & Rob Watson for their enduring support. Especial thanks to Drew Kennickell, my very own anchor, and Sebastian James Finlay Kennickell, my sun.

Earlier versions of some of these poems were previously published in *Broken Pencil*, *Contemporary Verse 2*, and in the chapbook *Phobic* (Gaspereau, 2006). Many thanks to the editors of each.

PHOTO: DREW KENNICKELL

ABOUT THE AUTHOR

Triny Finlay was born in Melbourne, Australia and grew up in Toronto. She is the author of *Splitting Off* (Nightwood, 2004), *Histories Haunt Us* (Nightwood, 2010), and the chapbook *Phobic* (Gaspereau, 2006). Her poetry has been anthologized in *Breathing Fire 2: Canada's New Poets*, *Qwerty Decade*, and *Gaspereau Gloriatur: Book of the Blessed Tenth Year*; her writing has also appeared in various Canadian periodicals. She has studied at Mount Allison University, the University of New Brunswick, and the University of Toronto. She lives with her family in Fredericton, NB, where she teaches English and Creative Writing at the University of New Brunswick.